Learn Club Jugglin Minutes

3 Club Juggling for adults & kids

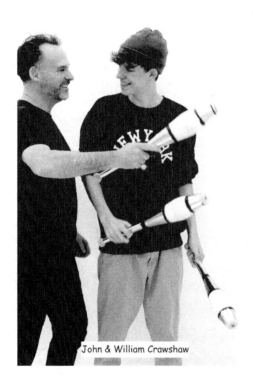

John & William Crawshaw

J A CRAWSHAW

Published by Xylem Publishing

Copyright@ 2022 J A Crawshaw

XYLEM
Publishing

This book and the author do not advocate minors juggling with fire.

The author has supplied information to the best of their knowledge and is constitutes their own beliefs and knowledge.

The 3 club cascade system can be achieved in 15 minutes or less, but the reading of the whole book first is highly recommended. Tricks will take longer.

Cover image by Shutter stock
Cover design by J A Crawshaw
Internal images (Juggling). William Crawshaw
Photography. Lewis Jordan

Introduction

Congratulations, you've taken the first steps to becoming a 'club' juggler.

You may have progressed from juggling balls or decided to jump straight in with clubs? Either way, juggling is a fantastic skill to have. Whether you are juggling alone, with friends, or as part of an organisation, juggling is truly international and unites people from all over the world.

By following the eight steps within this book and paying particular attention to the hints and tips, you could be juggling clubs within 15 minutes. This book is designed to introduce you to the regular three club cascade and learn all the practical moves in 15 minutes. However, I do recommend reading the entire book, so that you fully understand the process first, and ultimately speed up the learning process.

The whole book covers more detail, including troubleshooting issues, where to find more information, tricks and juggling with other equipment.

Juggling is a skill which needs practice, and the more you practice, the better you will become, that's a guarantee. One of my greatest tips for anyone learning for the first time is not to get frustrated if you're not progressing as quickly as you want. Instead, take your time and persevere. You are training your brain to do something it's never done before and that takes a little patience. One thing is for sure, the results can be mind-blowing.

Follow each step within the book carefully. Don't be frightened of going back to an earlier stage if you feel you need to. In fact, this is my greatest advice of all, and all the people I have taught have done better and progressed more quickly when they routinely go back to the previous step and nail it before moving on.

Okay, let's get straight to it.

Choosing The Right Clubs

What will you need? Juggling clubs come in many different shapes, sizes and colours, but usually consist of a handle and a weighted end. The weighted end tends to be bulbous, so making the handle more obvious and easier to spin.

Handle

Bulbous end

Protective foam 'stoppers' are to protect the ends from damage, should they be dropped on hard surfaces.

Below is a guide to choosing the right clubs for you. I recommend going to a juggling supplies store and try out the various possibilities before you buy. However, most beginners clubs are very similar in size and weight and can be successfully ordered online if that works for you? What's important, is to make sure they are the same shape and size. They are usually sold in packs of three, but obviously, more can be added should you require them.

Basic clubs   Radical Fish clubs   Euro style clubs

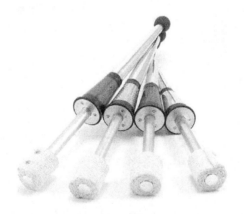

Fire torches

Basic clubs are ideal for beginners. Usually with softer handles and simple colouring, they will cope well with being regularly dropped on the floor.

Radical Fish clubs tend to suit a more advanced juggler. They are specifically weighted and designed for tricks.

Performance/Euro Style clubs can have brightly coloured sections which may be easily damaged if frequently dropped on hard surfaces.

All of the clubs above can be used by beginners. My advice is to choose clubs which appeal to you, so that you want to pick them up and use them.

Fire torches can potentially be very dangerous and restricted for adult use only. Restrictions on purchase may exist in your area and should be observed. These clubs are weighted differently from the 'normal' clubs and may take time to get used to. Notwithstanding an end which is on fire!

Attending a class or a club/association is a fantastic way to get access to different equipment and learn new skills. Juggling with other people is also great fun and an opportunity to keep up to date with new designs and techniques.

Speak with your local supplier to understand the choices available to you and discuss your needs and budget.

To follow this book, you will need three clubs of the same size and weight. You are also likely to be dropping them on the floor regularly as you learn, so choosing clubs which will be able to cope with this, is recommended.

Step 1. Position And Stance

At this stage, we are going to forget about the clubs. It's tempting to hold all three clubs in your hands and try to juggle them into the air. Like any other sport or activity, attaining the correct position and stance will help you greatly to achieve good results.

Put the clubs to one side and stand with your feet shoulder width apart so that you are comfortable and relaxed.

Flex slightly at the knees and keep your back straight. As usual with all beginners, there is a tendency to throw the clubs forward and flexing at the knees and keeping your back straight will help to prevent this from happening. This doesn't mean that you are bending over at the knees, but just flexing in a relaxed style, like on a skate or surf board. In fact, being relaxed is the key to success with juggling, and if you find yourself becoming too tense and rigid, then just stop, take time out and start again when you are ready.

Now, before we bring any clubs into the situation, I want you to hold your hands out with your elbows at 90° as if you were holding a tray or similar. Again, they should be shoulder width apart. Your hands are now in the perfect catching & release position. Remember to breathe.

In my opinion. breathing is one of the keys to success, It's tempting when learning a new skill to hold your breath until you've mastered a particular move, but breathing in a relaxed fashion

again will help you to achieve quicker and better results. What you will find, hopefully, is that the process of juggling in itself will help you to relax and your breathing will be calm. But to start off, be conscious of your breathing.

Step 2. First Club

Now take one club and hold it in your dominant hand. This is usually the hand you would use to write with, but you may feel comfortable with the opposite? It's up to you and do whatever feels natural.

Hold the clubs near to the middle of the handle. I prefer to hold it as shown below so that I can create spin on the club which is not too fast or too slow and it feels comfortable.

The club should be pointing away from you and the handle and end stopper able to move past your forearm, when you move the club up and down.

Start with the club near your hip and raise your arm to initiate the throw. The club should spin once at about chest height. It should be pointing at 45° to your body line, so that you can easily catch it in your other hand.

Return the club to your dominant hand. We will call this 'hand one' and your other, 'hand two'. With the club in hand one, throw it again so that it spins in front of you and then drops down into hand two and stop there.

Hints & tips for this section are not to spin it too quickly. The club shouldn't hurt your hand when you catch it. In addition, when you catch, try to follow through as if you are almost cushioning the fall. This will help later, when you have to throw it again to create a more continuous fluid action.

A good tip is to get your receiving hand ready for the catch and make sure it is aligned as shown below.

Now take the club in hand one and practise throwing to hand two and repeat this until it feels comfortable. It's important not to be tempted to rush into two or three clubs at this stage, but to work on the one club technique until you feel confident.

Now when you are comfortable catching the club in hand two, throw it from hand two back to hand one, so that the club spins once and then catch in hand one.

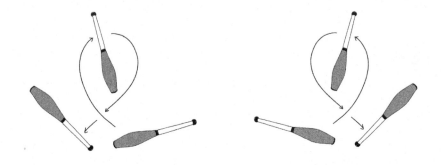

From right to left   From left to right

This may feel a little strange, as your dominant hand will feel more natural starting, but if you can master this move, then you have cracked juggling. Seriously! Because this is the only move you will need to do, to juggle one club, three clubs, five clubs etc. Getting this right from the start opens the gate for you to be a competent club juggler.

Again, practise this move over and over until you achieve a smooth rhythm.

At this point, you might not feel like you've made much progress, but really you should congratulate yourself. Because this is the only thing you need to do to juggle three clubs and you have established the fundamentals to moving forward to STEP 3. WELL DONE!

Step 3. Introducing The Second Club

Now take a club in hand one and another club in hand two. Throw club 1 from hand one as you have been doing in the previous step, making sure it rotates once and then drops down to hand two. Just before you catch it, you release club 2 up into the air and then catch it with hand one.

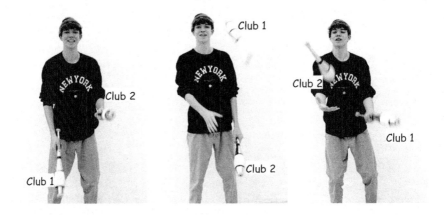

The tip here is to make sure that the outgoing club goes underneath the incoming club and not outside it, and time it so that they don't collide. Don't throw too early. In reality, you leave it almost to the last second, before you release.

18

Don't worry if you don't catch every club, this is common and again practice will make perfect. Go through the process again and again, making sure that you stay relaxed and that both clubs spin at the same speed. This is where you can start to count to create a rhythm.

'One and two and'. Count out loud as you throw and catch the clubs. Throw club 1 as you say 'one,' throw club 2 as you say 'and' then catch club 1 as you say 'two', then catch club 2 as you say 'and'.

The tip here is to count as slowly as you possibly can. The clubs will dictate the pace to some degree, but trying to control the rhythm by saying it as slowly as possible will give you more time when it comes to club number 3 later on.

Repeat this step until you are fluid. This is a critical stage, because most people feel the urge to get hold of the third club and try introducing it to the pattern. Don't. Stick with two clubs and practise this move until your brain is happy with it. Hints &

tips here are not to rush. Keep counting and the slower you can go, the better, trust me.

Concentrate on making a solid catch of club 1 while club 2 is in the air. Make it 'safe' and then quickly switch your focus to catching club 2.

Step 4. Two Club Juggling

Congratulations. If you are at this point, you are doing very well and are so close to pulling this off.

Start as you did in STEP 3 and this time, when you catch club 2, throw it again immediately as if you are repeating the original pattern and it becomes club 1. Keep this going so that you are effectively two club juggling. Remember to count, 'one and two and... one and two and... one and two and'. See how long you can keep going.

The tip here is to keep things slow and make your catches solid and secure.

Step 5. Practice

The key to introducing the 3rd club is to make sure your 2 club juggling is polished.

You will have been making regular drops and this is completely normal. Take time to reassure yourself that you're actually doing a fantastic job, and try not to get frustrated if things are not coming together as quickly as you thought. Practicing this step will provide a great foundation for moving on to step 6.

Step 6. Introducing The 3rd Club

Hold two clubs in your dominant hand (Hand one).

This is not easy and usually takes time to get used to it.

Hold the two clubs together as shown below.

Club 1 will be the one to the right as you look at this photo. It will be the one on the inside as you look at the clubs in your own hand.

The tip here is to make sure the handle and foam stopper are above the handle of club 2 and the bulbous end slightly below.

Now, make sure your stance has not 'tightened up' and that your legs are relaxed and flexing at the knees.

Start with the two clubs in your dominant hand and starting from around your thigh, bring your arm up and release club 1. In my opinion, this is probably the hardest bit to get right and again practicing this move, will enable you to be able to launch it into the air, complete a full spin and be able to catch it in hand two.

Don't worry too much about the other two clubs. It's good to have them ready, but concentrate on the release of club 1.

If you feel inclined to release club 2 in order to catch it, then go ahead. If not, just let club 1 fall to the floor and practice releasing club 1 and completing a full spin.

Take time now to get to the stage where you can comfortably catch club 1 having released club 2. When you are comfortable with this, move on to step 7.

Step 7. The Big One!

Stop for a minute and contemplate how far you have come. You are doing incredibly well and the next step is not as hard as you might think.

In fact, the next step is nothing new! You are not actually doing anything different to what you have done in Step 1. Club 3 is really just the same as club 1. You throw it exactly as you do club 1, from your dominant hand, complete one full spin as clubs 1 and 2 and then catch it.

Take a breath, keep your back straight and flex at the knees.

You can do this.

Timing is everything here, and what you have done in the previous steps will have prepared you well if you have kept things as slow as possible. If you find you haven't enough time to fit club 3 in, you're not throwing the clubs high enough or your hands have crept up slightly.

If you think you need more time? Go back through the previous steps and slow things down to create more time.

Ok. With two clubs in your dominant hand and one club in the other, start your first throw. Don't feel intimidated. You can do this, believe in yourself and see the pattern in front of you. Remember, there's nothing new now.

Club 1 is thrown and spins in front of you.

Just before you catch club 1, you throw club 2.

Just before you catch club 2, you throw club 3 and just before you catch it, you throw the club which is in that hand so you can make a solid catch.

Most people at this stage drop this club and that's natural. It feels so completely mad that you have just juggled.

Yes! You have just juggled three clubs. Give yourself a pat on the back and keep your cool. Because, you're going to do it again.

The tip here is to make a solid catch of club 3 and don't worry too much about catching club 4. This will come. Remember, you've done it before.

You have now completed the seven steps you need to juggle three clubs. Keep practising and don't be afraid of going back a step. People who go back to refresh a previous step, tend to progress quicker in the long run. It's actually worth the time investment, even if it feels like a backwards step.

The question now is? How do you stop!
A clean finish without all the clubs ending up on the floor will complete the pattern with style.

Move on to step 8.

Step 8. The Double Spin Finish

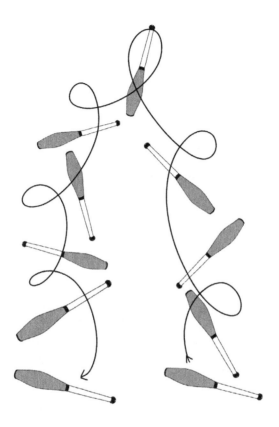

The double spin finish looks great and is reasonably easy to accomplish.

Firstly, start by practicing with just one club. Throw the club high in front of you from your favoured hand and instead of it completing one full revolution, it completes two before you catch it in the other hand.

Practice until you are taking solid catches every time. I doesn't matter if sometimes you have to lower your body or kneel on one knee to make the catch, because this can make it look even better when you finish your routine.

The tip here is to not spin it too quickly. It will be difficult to catch and there won't be enough time to do the next bit.

So, you're juggling with three clubs and you're preparing in your mind to make the finish.
Make your decision on which club you will throw. It will be from the hand, as you have been practicing.

Make the double spin throw and then immediately pass the club which is in the catching had to the other. While the club is spinning, you now have two clubs in the non catching hand and you've stopped juggling. Now, keep your eye on the spinning club and make the catch as you practiced.

Ta Da. It looks neat and fancy. You can now take your bow.

Troubleshooting

Problem	Reason	Things to try
Walking forward	You're walking forward because you're throwing the clubs slightly forward	Don't hunch forwards Don't let your wrists drop Flex at your knees
Breaking concentration due to picking the clubs off the floor	Breaking your stance and concentration as you routinely pick up clubs is common	Try juggling next to a bed or sofa. Now the clubs are more easily reached
Missing a solid catch	The clubs are bouncing off or missing your hand	Choose clubs which feel right for you. Go back a step and practice the catch. Slow the spin speed. Where you look is vital. Concentrate on the whole picture and not the catches specifically
Not enough time to get club 3 into the mix	Clubs 1 and 2 are moving too quickly	Throw the clubs higher to create more time. Try widening your arms
Struggling to throw the first club when 2 in your hand	Club 1 trapped under club 3. No momentum	Make sure club 1 is clear of club 3. Start your throw from around thigh height, bring your entire arm up and flick with your wrist

Chasing the clubs	Inconsistent throws	This is very common when learning. Try concentrating on a uniform pattern where each club goes the same height and their speed is consistent. Keep your body aligned and your hands level with each other
Can't seem to progress	There may be many reasons	Rushing and wanting to progress faster than you are able is very common. Slow down and don't be afraid to invest in going back to a previous step. You may be in the wrong environment. Find somewhere quiet and with space. Try to think about juggling and nothing else
Feeling mentally & physically exhausted	It is possible to overdo it! Juggling can involve huge shifts in thinking and physical activity	Take a break and don't think you have to be a competent juggler the first time you do it. Often taking breaks and coming back to it fresh helps you progress faster

Reflecting And Moving On

The freedom of continual juggling can be an extremely exhilarating experience. Let your mind enjoy the process. You might find that it becomes so natural that you can switch off to everything around you and use juggling to relax and even meditate.

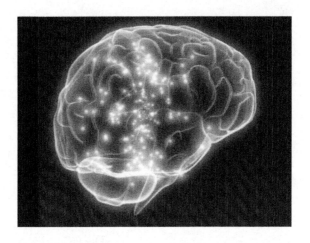

The more you improve, the easier it will become, and you will stop focussing on throwing and catching and more on the holistic pattern. In a way, it becomes instinctive, like riding a bike or driving a car.

It's been proven that juggling can bring together both sides of the brain and, in doing so, allows your brain to relax. It feels great, and I know many people who use juggling to relax, clear their thoughts and even meditate. As I do.

This could be very useful, before an important exam or interview or if you're just feeling stressed or anxious. At the end of the day, juggling is a fun thing to do. Enjoy your juggling and see where it takes you.

You could even make a career out of it.

No matter how good you become, dropping the clubs is something that will always happen, so don't beat yourself up about it. Street entertainers and performers actually incorporate a drop into part of the show if it happens. Or, they simply pick it up and continue without making a big fuss. Believe me, people who can't juggle will be impressed anyway.

Enjoy your juggling. You're now in a very unique club. The world is your oyster and clubs are just the start. There are also many other books which go into much more detail and even scientific study into the health benefits and cognitive effects of juggling if you want to delve deeper. This book is designed to introduce you to the wonderful world of juggling and not an attempt to blind you with science, but it's out there if you want it.

There are also many social media groups and juggling influencers, who offer more detailed information and ideas. Best of all, there is nothing better than getting together with other jugglers and exchanging ideas and experiences. It has happened to me all over the world, from beaches to nightclubs, where someone spotted me juggling or vice versa. You never know. You might be able to teach someone else with your new-found skill.

Enjoy!

Tricks With Clubs

You might have zoomed through this book so quickly and easily that you are already thinking about incorporating tricks into your pattern?

This, of course, can be done. With the same amount of practice and determination, anything is possible.

Overhand Spin

Instead of initiating the spin with palm upwards, try taking a club and turn your wrist over, so that you undertake a backhand movement. This will enable you to align the club with your body and spin it across the front of you. The change in angle looks great when done every 3rd club or so.

Reverse Spin

This manoeuvre involves a lot of practice. Have your hands and the club in the same position as normal, but instead of pushing the bulbous end up to form the spin. Push the handle up and rotate away from you. Give it a try. It looks great, and again can be done with every 3rd club or if you really want to go for it, each and every club.

Double Spin

Incorporating a double spin makes the club go higher and looks amazing. It's a good one to learn when you start introducing tricks, because it is the same as the double spin ending. Only this time, you keep going. Try putting one double spin in every now and then and progress to every club.

Triple Spin

As above, but really go for it with a triple rotation. Keep your eye on the handle and be flexible in your stance, so that you can anticipate the incoming club and move accordingly. Also a great finish.

Palm Spin

Hold the club as you would hold a pencil, with the handle pointing to you. Have the club to rest on your middle finger for support.

Initiate the spin with your wrist and index finger, then open out your hand flat, so that the club spins freely. Allow it to complete a full 360°, then take the handle as normal ready to throw it back into the cascade.

This trick is best carried out in the time gap a double spin provides.

Chops

The chop is the exaggerated downward movement of a club which stays in your hand.

Undertake an underarm throw. Toss the 'underarm' club so that it spins as normal. At the same time, maintain grip on the club with the hand of the arm you're going under. Raise the arm so that your elbow is at 90^0 and quickly initiate the sharp and exaggerated downward movement to around waist height.

The action is much like what you would do to try and shake off imaginary water from the club.

Then release the club in a 'normal' toss back into the cascade and very quickly indeed, catch the club which originally went under the arm.

This is a very quick movement and will require much practice. Separating the movements will help. Practice the underarm throw first, and then introduce the chop without trying to carry on juggling. When you are proficient at the move, go ahead and integrate it into your normal cascade pattern.

Under The Leg

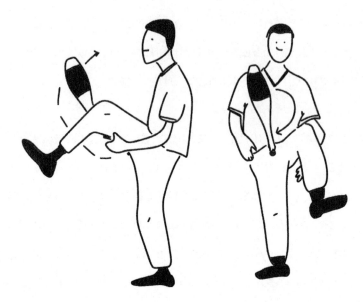

Including a throw under one leg within your cascade routine can look impressive. I suggest starting with the leg on the same side as the arm which will make the throw.

In the picture above, left arm, left leg or vice versa.

The tip here is to raise your knee as high as you can, so you're not having to reach too low and waste valuable time.

The key to success is to start raising your knee slightly before you catch the club which will go under it.

Toss the club under the leg so it spins high enough to be incorporated back into your cascade.

Juggling With Fire

Fire juggling is strictly for adults only.

DISCLAIMER: the author takes no responsibility for any injury, loss or damage occurring as a result of using the information which follows. Fire clubs are basically juggling clubs to which you set fire to one end.

Juggling fire can be very dangerous. I recommend practicing with the clubs unlit, until you are proficient. Only juggle fire if you have adequate outdoor space away from combustible material.

Safety Points:
- Juggle fire clubs under the supervision of someone with experience
- Use your common sense
- Tie back hair
- Become proficient at juggling the clubs unlit first
- Avoid windy days
- Practice on ground which will not catch fire if you drop them
- Never attempt to catch the lit end. Simply let it fall to the floor
- Never use petrol. Petrol is extremely flammable and could cause serious injury. Paraffin is usually used and just enough to soak the wick
- Don't allow the fuel to spill. If so, clean up immediately.
- Be careful doing tricks as the flame may just catch you out

A Bit About The Author

John Crawshaw has been juggling since he was about 10 years old, when he picked fruit out of the fruit bowl and taught himself. He cost his mum a fortune in bruised apples and oranges, but progressed to balls as a teenager. Joining the Cosmos Juggling Club in York, England in 1992, where he learned to juggle clubs, knives and perform tricks with other jugglers. He set up the university juggling club at The University of Humberside and performed on an amateur basis at fetes and fundraising events.

To earn extra money, while at university, he taught people on the street to juggle in 15 minutes and that's where the inspiration for this book and others came from.

A sufferer of dyslexia, he found juggling to be an immense help to his brain, when often he would become stressed or confused. Juggling somehow managed to help. In 2021 at the age of 52 he wrote 'The Void Between Words', his memoir and personal journey of battling with dyslexia and associated mental health issues. Juggling features significantly within the book and is highly recommended if you want to find out more about how juggling can help you with learning difficulties and focussing your brain. (Link at the end of this book).

He is not a professional juggler, but juggling has remained a hobby to which he is very grateful. He hopes this book might at least introduce you to the wonderful world of juggling, but moreover, encourage you to see that you could acquire a new skill, and that anything is possible.

8 Reasons Why Juggling Is Good For You

1. Juggling boosts brain development. Research indicates that learning to juggle accelerates the growth of neural connections related to memory, focus, movement, and vision. The beneficial changes persist even after weeks without practice.

2. Juggling doesn't discriminate by age, size, gender, race, religion or athletic ability. Anyone can be a fantastic juggler.

3. Juggling builds hand-eye coordination in ways that improve reaction time, reflexes, spatial awareness, strategic thinking, and concentration. This helps improve confidence as well as athletic ability. It may, also, even promote reading skills

4. Juggling gets you moving enough to increase your oxygen intake.

5. Juggling can be stimulating as well as calming. While learning more complicated juggling skills you rely on left-brain processes, carefully focusing and analysing the steps. When practicing skills you've

already mastered you rely on right-brained processes, relaxing into a more fluid, intuitive motion. The bringing together of both sides, can be a very powerful thing.

6. Juggling puts you in charge, since you can make it as easy or difficult as you choose. Start with three clubs. To ramp up the challenge increase the speed, add more clubs, or change patterns. You can also change props, learn trick juggling, try multi-person juggling or go for the chainsaws!

7. Juggling teaches a growth mindset. You learn from mistakes, noticing how effort and increasing experience bring you ever greater mastery.

8. Juggling is incredible fun.

More Information

The Complete Juggler by Dave Finnigan

Juggling With Finesse by Kit Summers

International Jugglers Association.

https://www.juggle.org

European Juggling Association.

https://www.eja.net

My memoir 'The Void Between Words' can be found on Amazon, in bookstores and other digital platforms. Find out how juggling helped me to overcome my learning difficulties.

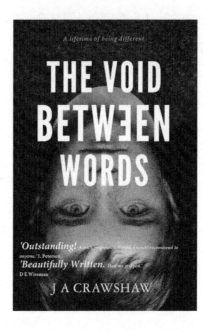

https://www.amazon.co.uk/dp/183837731X

https://www.amazon.com/Void-Between-Words-lifetime-different/dp/183837731X

If you have found this book useful? I would be incredibly grateful if you would spare two minutes to write a review on the relevant platform.

Good reviews help others access the book and help us to spread the positivity and health benefits of juggling to others.

Instagram: J_A_Crawshaw_Author

Don't forget to leave a review & let us know how long it took you to juggle 3 clubs

XYLEM
Publishing

Other titles of interest?

Printed in Great Britain
by Amazon

16535138R00031